KWAME NKRUMAH:

WARRIOR KING

NANCY LOEWEN
SENCHI FERRY LIBRARY

Text Copyright © 2026 Planting People Growing Justice Press
Illustrations copyright © 2026 Planting People Growing Justice Press

Cover Artwork and Illustrations by Whimsical Designs by CJ
Design by Reyhana Ismail

All rights reserved.

No part of this book may be reproduced in any manner without express written consent of the publisher, except in the case of brief excerpts in critical reviews and articles.

All inquiries or sales request should be addressed to:

Planting People Growing Justice Press
P.O. Box 131894
Saint Paul, MN 55113
www.ppgjli.org

Manufactured in Dongguan, China by R.R. Donnelley
First Edition
LCCN: 2025937749
1-9798896050117/9798896050124-07/15/2025

TABLE OF CONTENTS

Introduction
Free Forever! 4

Chapter 1:
Always Learning 7

Chapter 2:
From Africa to America 10

Chapter 3:
Warrior King 15

Chapter 4:
Claiming Freedom 20

Ways to Make a Difference 24

About the Author 26

Glossary 28

Source Notes, Books, Websites 30

Words in **bold** are in the glossary.

FREE FOREVER!

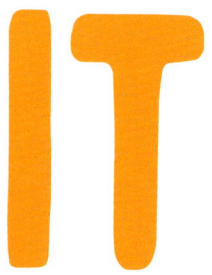**IT** is March 7, 1957.

At midnight, a British flag is lowered to the ground. A new flag goes up in its place. A band plays a lively song as an excited crowd watches.

For more than 100 years, Africa has been in the grip of European colonialism. Now Ghana has become the first African nation to declare its independence.

A man in traditional dress speaks to the crowd from a balcony.

"At long last, the battle has ended!" declares the man. His voice holds power and joy. "Ghana, your beloved country is free forever!"

The crowd cheers wildly.

The man speaking is Prime Minister Kwame Nkrumah. He has worked tirelessly to reach the goal of freedom for Ghana. Now, at long last, this dream has been realized.

But Nkrumah has even bigger dreams. He wants freedom not just for Ghana, but for *every* African nation. He believes in a free and united Africa. Nkrumah's vision will have a lasting impact on Africa and on the entire world.

COLONIALISM IN AFRICA

The Gold Coast (now Ghana) was ruled by Great Britain from 1821 to 1957 in a practice called colonialism.

This is when one country takes control of another country, usually to claim the area's minerals, crops, or other resources. The people in the colonized country are not allowed to govern themselves.

At one time, all of Africa except for Liberia and Ethiopia was under colonial rule by European countries such as Great Britain, France, Portugal, Spain, and Italy.

CHAPTER 1:
ALWAYS LEARNING

Kwame Nkrumah was born on September 21, 1909, in the Gold Coast village of Nkroful. He lived there with his mother until he was three. Then they moved to join his father, a goldsmith, in the town of Half Assini, about fifty miles away.

Kwame was from a big family. He was his mother's only child, but he had many brothers and sisters. There was always someone to play with. But what Nkrumah liked best was to wander off on his own. He loved to sit quietly and watch birds and animals. Sometimes he tried to bring them home as pets.

Nkrumah's mother did not have an education, but she valued learning. She insisted that Nkrumah go to school. Nkrumah attended a one-room schoolhouse with students of all ages. Nkrumah did not like school at first. He ran away on his first day. But his mother kept taking him back each morning. Soon Nkrumah learned to love school.

When Nkrumah was seventeen years old, he worked as a student teacher for a year. One day, the principal of a teacher training college visited his classroom. He was so impressed with Nkrumah that he arranged for Nkrumah to attend his college.

At the Government Training College in Accra, Nkrumah studied, ran track, learned tribal drumming, and took part in theater and debate. He graduated in 1930. He later said those were among his happiest days.

CHAPTER 2:
FROM AFRICA TO AMERICA

Nkrumah's first job out of college was teaching kindergarten. His young students became very attached to him.

Next, Nkrumah worked as the head teacher at a Roman Catholic school for two years. He soon realized that he did not just want to teach. He wanted to keep learning. And not just anywhere. He wanted to go to school in the United States. He had his heart set on Lincoln University in Pennsylvania.

With financial help from a family member, he made plans to leave Africa. His mother cried when he told her he was leaving, but she insisted that he go. "May God and your ancestors guide you," she said.

Nkrumah studied in the United States for ten years. He earned degrees in economics, sociology, and theology from Lincoln University. He also earned master's degrees in education and philosophy from the University of Pennsylvania.

To support himself, Nkrumah worked at many jobs. He worked in a library, a shipyard, a soap factory, and in ships at sea. He also preached and became known as an effective speaker.

The time Nkrumah spent in America helped shape his views about freedom and equality. He read books by important thinkers such as Marcus Garvey and W.E.B. Du Bois. He understood the struggles of poor people because of his own financial struggles. He saw for himself how Black people were treated unfairly because of their skin color. These experiences gave Nkrumah a strong desire to see African nations unite and work together.

FACT: EDUCATION FOR CHANGE

Lincoln University is a historically Black university that was founded in 1854. It was the first historically Black college or university (HBCU) to grant college degrees. Supreme Court Justice Thurgood Marshall, renowned Harlem Renaissance poet Langston Hughes, and famous jazz singer Cab Calloway attended Lincoln University.

In May 1945, Nkrumah headed to London, England to study law. Leaving New York City by ship, he looked back at the Statue of Liberty. She seemed to be waving to him personally. "You have opened my eyes to the true meaning of liberty," he thought. "I shall never rest until I have carried your message to Africa."

In London, he became a leader in a powerful organization for West African students. The group helped students with practical matters like housing and jobs. It also pushed for better conditions in West Africa.

Later that year, in October 1945, Nkrumah helped manage the fifth **Pan-African** Congress in Manchester, England. Activists gathered from around the world. They talked about putting an end to colonial rule. Nkrumah was a key speaker. He gave inspiring speeches about **self-determination** and economic independence. His vision of a united Africa was beginning to take hold.

SOURCES OF INSPIRATION

Marcus Garvey (1887-1940) was an important Black leader in the early 1900s. He promoted Black pride, unity, and **economic independence**. He influenced many leaders, including Malcolm X and Martin Luther King, Jr.

W.E.B. Du Bois (1868-1963) was an intellectual and an activist who helped shape the civil rights movement. He was the first Black person to earn a Ph.D. from Harvard University. In 1909, he co-founded the National Association for the Advancement of Colored People (NAACP).

CHAPTER 3:
WARRIOR KING

In 1947, Nkrumah returned to the Gold Coast (now Ghana). He had been asked to be the secretary of a group called the United Gold Coast Convention (UGCC). This group was working to achieve independence from British rule.

Back home, Nkrumah saw his mother for the first time in twelve years. At first, she did not think it was him. While he was in the United States, the gap between his teeth had been fixed. But then she recognized his hands and knew he was her son.

Nkrumah traveled all across the country. He set up schools and UGCC offices. His old car often broke down. His suitcase held nothing more than two suits, two pairs of shoes, and some underclothes. But everywhere he went, his speeches got people excited about their future.

In 1948, British police killed two men during a peaceful demonstration. Riots broke out. Nkrumah

and other UGCC leaders were arrested for stirring up violence. For weeks, Nkrumah lived alone in a hut, guarded by police. Every night he was visited by a mongoose (an animal similar to a weasel). He later wrote that this was the first time in thirteen years that he could be alone with his thoughts.

Nkrumah became frustrated with the UGCC. He felt that progress was happening too slowly. In 1949, he formed a party called the Convention People's Party (CPP). The CPP called for immediate independence from Great Britain. The new party quickly became very popular.

Nkrumah launched the Positive Action Campaign in January 1950. People **boycotted** British goods.

FACT: CONNECTING WITH THE PEOPLE

Nkrumah started a newspaper called the *Accra Evening News* in 1948. He used the paper to keep people informed about the fight for freedom. The paper helped unite the people of the Gold Coast.

They held mass protests. Transportation workers held **strikes**. Daily life nearly came to a standstill.

A few weeks after the Positive Action Campaign began, Nkrumah was arrested and put into prison. But the CPP kept getting stronger. A year later, in February 1951, the Gold Coast held its first general election. The CPP swept the polls. Nkrumah won a seat in Parliament, the lawmaking body of the government. He was released from prison. In 1952, he became prime minister (head of Parliament).

Nkrumah and the CPP continued to fight for independence. Finally, their efforts paid off. In March 1957, the Gold Coast and a territory called Togoland were merged into a new nation. Nkrumah himself picked the name of Ghana. It means "warrior king" in the Soninke language.

In his famous midnight speech, Nkrumah said the words so many people had been longing to hear: "Ghana is free forever!"

LIKE-MINDED LEADERS

American **civil rights** leader Martin Luther King, Jr. attended the celebration of Ghana's independence. Both King and Nkrumah believed in using nonviolent methods to achieve change. They drew inspiration from Mahatma Gandhi, who had led India to freedom from British rule ten years earlier. Like Gandhi, they used peaceful protest and **civil disobedience** to fight for freedom, human rights, and justice.

CHAPTER 4:
CLAIMING FREEDOM

More changes were in store for the government of Ghana. In 1960, the people of Ghana approved a new **constitution**. Ghana no longer had a parliamentary system with a prime minister. It became a **republic**. People could vote directly for their president, as in the United States. The president would have a great deal of power.

Nkrumah was elected as Ghana's first president. He was eager to turn Ghana into a modern, wealthy country. He built roads, railways, and ports. He built schools, hospitals, and factories. One of his most important contributions was the Akosombo Dam on the Volta River. The dam provided hydroelectric power for Ghana's new industries.

Nkrumah wanted Ghana to advance quickly. He believed the best way to do that was to keep more power in the hands of the government. But his approach created problems. Ghana borrowed a lot of money from other countries. The economy became weak. Many people felt their concerns weren't being heard.

> **FACT: THE COLORS OF GHANA**
>
> On the Ghanaian flag, red stands for the struggle for independence. Yellow stands for the country's wealth. Green stands for its forests and farms. The black star stands for the guiding principle of freedom.

In 1966, Nkrumah's presidency came to an end. A group of military officers and politicians removed him from office. Nkrumah was no longer allowed to live in Ghana, so he moved to Guinea. He died of cancer on April 27, 1972.

In spite of the challenges of his later years, Nkrumah left behind an important legacy. He inspired many other countries to pursue freedom. At one time, all of Africa was under colonial rule except for Liberia and Ethiopia. Today, every African nation is free.

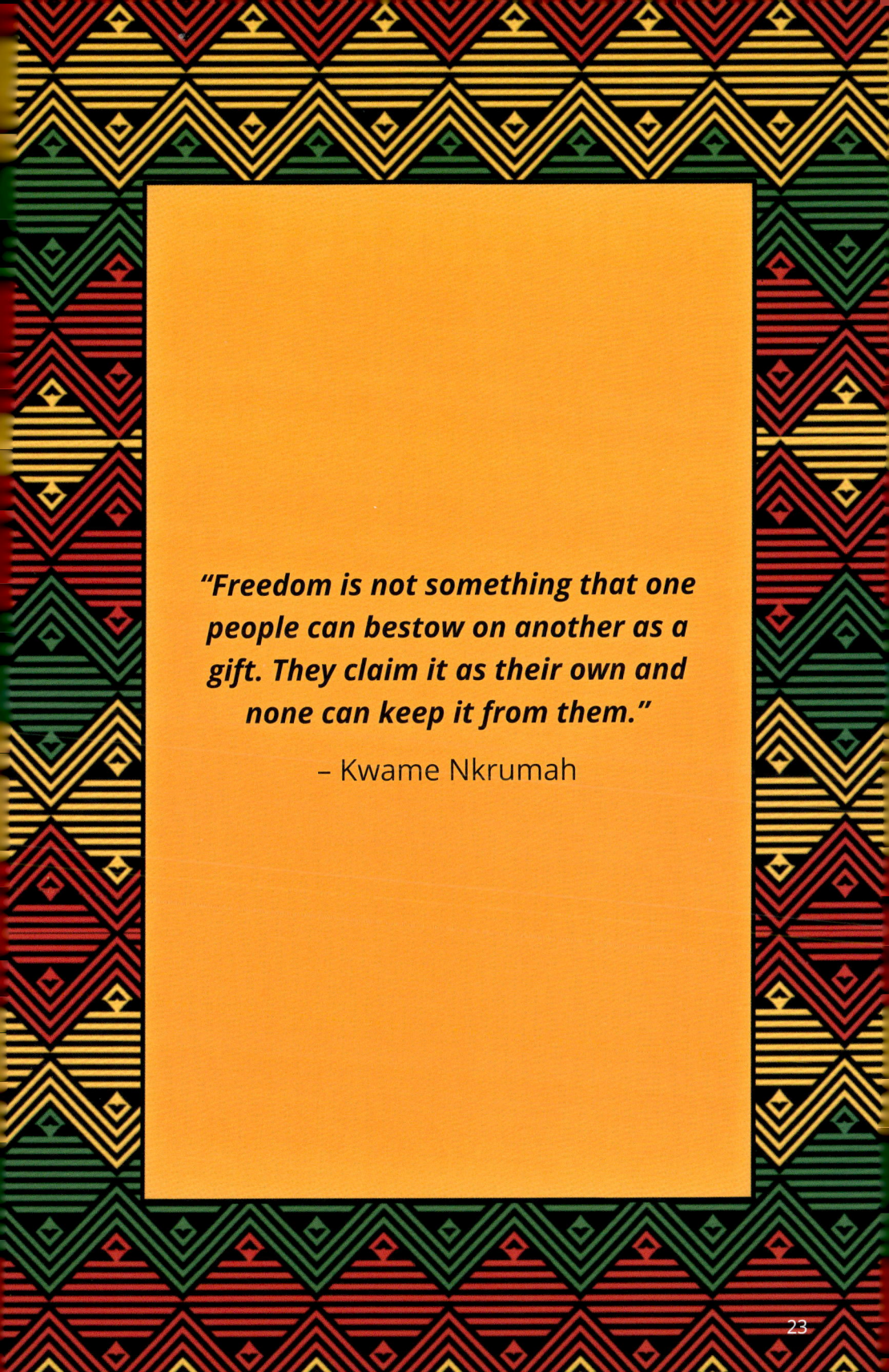

"Freedom is not something that one people can bestow on another as a gift. They claim it as their own and none can keep it from them."

– Kwame Nkrumah

MAKING A DIFFERENCE

Learn all you can. Kwame Nkrumah studied many subjects. He tried to learn all he could from the people around him whether or not he agreed with them. His knowledge gave him confidence and a sense of direction.

Stay focused on your goals. Nkrumah had many talents. He could have worked in any number of professions. But nothing was more important to him than independence for Ghana. His determination and drive allowed him to accomplish great things.

Be willing to take risks. Going to the United States to study couldn't have been easy for Nkrumah. He had to adjust to a different culture. He was far away from his family and friends. But he was so committed to his education that he left behind the comforts of home. He believed in his own ability to adapt.

Stand up for what you believe in. Nkrumah didn't hesitate to say what was on his mind. He wasn't worried about winning the approval of others. He put his energy into stating his opinions clearly. He was persuasive, winning people over to create change.

Develop your writing skills. Nkrumah was always writing, whether it was papers for school or essays and speeches related to Ghana's independence. His writings had an enormous impact on his success. If you want to become a good writer, the first step is to read all you can. Really pay attention to writing that works well. How do writers keep the attention of their readers? Write as much as you can. The more you write, the better you will become.

Develop your speaking skills. Not many of us will give history-making speeches like Nkrumah did, but we all have something to say. Have you heard a speaker you really admire? Do any of your heroes have speeches that have been posted online? Study what they do. Then practice, practice, practice!

ABOUT THE AUTHORS

Nancy Loewen grew up on a farm in southwestern Minnesota, surrounded by library books and cats. She now lives in Saint Paul and has published more than 140 children's books, including *Charlotte E. Ray* and *Lusia Harris* in the PPGJ Difference Makers series.

The Senchi Ferry Community Library is dedicated to promoting literacy and advancing STEM education. The following students participated in a writing workshop led by Dr. Artika Tyner and proudly authored this book:

Ameku Saviour, Rhoda Ntow, Rachael Ntow, Sheila Nanna, Erica Agyeibea, Amoah Aikins, Kisseh Daniella, Gladys Matsiador, Kplorlanye Precious, Fekpey Iyvone, Bosi Newel, Joseph Ansah, Ahlijah Prince, Pascal Asante, Abigail Asare, Gadah Priscilla, Awuku Dorothy, Jocelyn Nyarkoa, Zia Alambel, Etornam Ndor, Emmanuel Ansah

GLOSSARY

Boycott	Refusing to buy something in order to make a point.
Civil Disobedience	Purposely disobeying laws that a person believes to be unfair.
Civil Rights	Basic rights and freedoms that every person should have. These rights include being able to go to school, vote, and speak freely.
Constitution	A set of basic laws that a country uses to govern itself. It sets up the structure of the government.
Economic Independence	When a country can take care of itself without needing a lot of help from other countries. The country has enough food and energy for its own people.
Pan-African	The idea that all people of African descent, no matter where they live in the world, are connected and should work together.

Republic	A type of government in which people vote directly for their leaders. These leaders then make decisions and create laws for the country.
Self-Determination	The freedom people have to decide for themselves what their government should be.
Strike	When workers stop working at the same time and refuse to go back to work until they get the change they are asking for.

BOOKS

Kyereme, E. & Sanusi, A. (2022). *AMA in Ghana*. Jireh Press.

Perkins, U. E. & Freeman, L. (2021). *Kwame Nkrumah's Midnight Speech for Independence*. Just Us Books.

Timelines from Black History: Leaders, Legends, Legacies. (2020). DK Publishing.

WEBSITES

Ghanaian Museum
https://ghanaianmuseum.com/

Britannica Kids
https://kids.britannica.com/students/article/Kwame-Nkrumah/276110#:~:text=One%20of%20the%20outstanding%20leaders,Gold%20Coast%2C%20in%20September%201909.

Kiddle
https://kids.kiddle.co/Kwame_Nkrumah

KidzSearch/Encyclopedia for Kids
https://wiki.kidzsearch.com/wiki/Kwame_Nkrumah

SOURCES

Encyclopedia Britannica, Inc. (2024, August 28). Kwame Nkrumah. Encyclopedia Britannica.
https://www.britannica.com/biography/Kwame-Nkrumah.

The Hutchins Center for African & African American Research. (n.d.). W. E. B. Du Bois.
https://hutchinscenter.fas.harvard.edu/web-dubois.

Independence speech – Kwame Nkrumah March 6, 1957, Accra, Ghana. Pan-African Quotes. (2012, March 10).
https://panafricanquotes.wordpress.com/speeches/independence-speech-kwame-nkrumah-march-6-1957-accra-ghana/.

National Archives and Records Administration. (n.d.). Marcus Garvey (August 17, 1887 - June 10, 1940).
https://www.archives.gov/research/african-americans/individuals/marcus-garvey.

New York Public Library. (2024, August 23). Research guides: Kwame Nkrumah Resource Guide: Kwame Nkrumah Biography.
https://libguides.nypl.org/kwamenkrumah/biography.

Nkrumah, K. (2023). Ghana: The Autobiography of Kwame Nkrumah. Echo Point Books & Media, LLC.

Stanford University. (n.d.). Nkrumah, Kwame. The Martin Luther King, Jr. Research and Education Institute.
https://kinginstitute.stanford.edu/nkrumah-kwame.

ABOUT PLANTING PEOPLE GROWING JUSTICE LEADERSHIP INSTITUTE

Planting People Growing Justice Leadership Institute seeks to plant seeds of social change through education, training, and community outreach.

All proceeds from this book will support the educational programming of Planting People Growing Justice Leadership Institute.